BEGINNER'S GUIDE TO INVESTING

INVESTING FOR TOMORROW

Discover Proven Strategies To Trade and Invest In Any Type of Market

Sam Pierce

Copyright © 2020 Sam Pierce

All Rights Reserved

Copyright 2020 By Sam Pierce - All rights reserved.

The following book is produced below with the goal of providing information that is as accurate and reliable as possible. Regardless, purchasing this eBook can be seen as consent to the fact that both the publisher and the author of this book are in no way experts on the topics discussed within and that any recommendations or suggestions that are made herein are for entertainment purposes only. Professionals should be consulted as needed prior to undertaking any of the action endorsed herein.

This declaration is deemed fair and valid by both the American Bar Association and the Committee of Publishers Association and is legally binding throughout the United States.

Furthermore, the transmission, duplication or reproduction of any of the following work including specific information will be considered an illegal act irrespective of if it is done electronically or in print. This extends to creating a secondary or tertiary copy of the work or a recorded copy and is only allowed with express written consent from the Publisher. All additional right reserved.

The information in the following pages is broadly considered to be a truthful and accurate account of facts and as such any inattention, use or misuse of the information in question by the reader will render any resulting actions solely under their purview. There are no scenarios in which the publisher or the original author of this work can be in any fashion deemed liable for any hardship or damages that may befall them after undertaking information described herein.

Additionally, the information in the following pages is intended only for informational purposes and should thus be thought of as universal. As befitting its nature, it is presented without assurance regarding its prolonged validity or interim quality. Trademarks that are mentioned are done without written consent and can in no way be considered an endorsement from the trademark holder.

Table of Contents

PART I 8

Chapter 1: Understanding the Fundamentals of Position Trading 9

    Difference Between Position Trading and Swing/Day Trading 9

    Reasons for Investing Long-Term 11

    Advantages of Long-Term Investing 12

    Drawbacks of Long-Term Investing 13

    Stocks to Hold for Long-Term 14

Chapter 2: Fundamentals of Position Trading 16

    Use of Technical Analysis and Fundamental Analysis in Position Trading 16

    Long-Term Investment Instruments 18

    Identifying Long-Term Trend 20

    Ignoring Short-Term Gains 21

    Spotting Long-Term Breakouts 23

Chapter 3: Building Wealth Through Position Trading 23

    Protection Against Shifts in the Market 25

    Diversification Against Risk 25

    Maintaining a Balanced Portfolio 26

PART II 29

Chapter 1: Understanding the Fundamentals of Swing Trading 30

    The Difference Between Swing Trading and Day Trading 31

    Advantages of Swing Trading 32

    Characteristics of a Swing Trader 33

    Conducting Research as a Swing Trader 35

Benefits and Drawbacks of Swing Trading 36

Swing Trading Assets 39

Chapter 2: Essentials of Swing Trading 42

Technical Analysis Tools Used in Swing Trading 43

The Use of Charts and Graphs 44

Use of Moving Average (MACD) 46

Significant Levels 49

Trend Continuation 50

The Head and Shoulders Pattern 51

Triple Tops and Triple Bottoms 53

Candlestick Analysis 54

"Timing" entry and exit points 55

Chapter 3: Risk Management in Swing Trading 57

Protecting Yourself Against Risk 57

Psychology in Swing Trading 59

Fundamental Analysis 60

Backtesting Strategies 61

Chapter 1: Understanding the Fundamentals of Day Trading 64

Characteristics of a Day Trader 66

Day Trading as a Full-Time Career 67

The Difference Between Day, Swing, and Position Trading 68

Benefits of Day Trading 70

Drawbacks of Day Trading 71

Day Trading Equities 72

Day Trading Options 74

Day Trading FOREX 75

Chapter 2: Essentials of Day Trading 76

Opening a New Brokerage Account 77

Placing Your First Trades 80

Best Time to Trade 82

Risk Management 83

Golden Rules of Money Management 85

Basic Technical Analysis Tools for Day Traders 86

Using the moving average to enter and exit a trade 88

Chapter 3: Choosing the Best Stocks for Your Portfolio 90

Company Financials 90

Earnings Per Share 92

Return on Equity 93

Analyst Recommendations 93

Other Financial Indicators 96

Conclusion 98

PART I

Chapter 1: Understanding the Fundamentals of Position Trading

There are investors who get into investing for the long haul. These are long-term investors, and their approach is known as "position trading." Position trading is a long-term approach that looks to engage in holding on to assets for an extended period of time. If you are patient and in no hurry to make quick profits, you may consider position trading as an option for you.

Position is a logical progression from swing trading. The reason for this is that it takes quite a bit of foresight to determine what a stock will do in six months' time. That takes a lot of research and understanding of the market. If you are unfamiliar with the dynamics of a given market or the companies that comprise it, you may have a hard time "timing" the movements of these stocks or assets.

Difference Between Position Trading and Swing/Day Trading

Position trading differs from day and swing trading insofar as the timeframe that positions remain open. To give you a parameter of comparison, day trading refers to opening and closing positions within the same trading day. Swing trading generally implies keeping positions open for roughly a week at a time. As for position trading, the usual yardstick is anything beyond 10 days to approximately 200 days. The reason for this parameter is the moving averages that are calculated. Based on this consideration, position investors look at the 20, 50, and 100-day moving average.

Based on the parameters offered by these moving averages, position investors can then determine how long they plan to keep their positions open based on the anticipated shifts in price action. However, if the investor sees that their anticipated movements happen sooner, they may be perfectly willing to liquidate their position earlier than expected.

For instance, a position investor anticipates that a stock will double in price in a period of about three months. However, the company performed better than expected, which led to them doubling their share price in two months. A savvy position investor would cash out at this time. Sure, greed might kick in at this point, thus tempting the investor to stay in longer. However, there is no telling what could happen beyond the anticipated price point. So, it's best to cash out and then consider taking up another position, this time at a higher price point.

This type of assessment is made not just on the technical data that you find in charts. It's also made as a result of a combination of fundamental analysis and other specific data on the company. Position investors like to get as much information as they can on companies. They'll even go as far as trying to talk to people on the inside to see what's going on.

This is why position investing is a very serious deal.

Reasons for Investing Long-Term

Long-term investing boils down to two factors. The first is maximizing profit as much as possible. The second is preserving wealth.

Let's look at the first reason.

Position investors are keen on making large profits on individual deals. They are not keen on making short-term profits. In the short-term, you stand to make pennies on the dollar. That's not bad, especially if you engage in high-frequency trading. But when it comes to hitting home runs, you have to stay in the game long enough. For instance, you cannot expect a company's stock price to double in a matter of hours. But, you can expect it to double in a matter of weeks. As a result, you stand to clean up is something like this happens.

The second reason is preserving wealth. Often, investors find themselves with extra cash. Having extra cash can be a problem, especially if it's not producing anything. Now, it's one thing to have an emergency savings fund that's sitting there waiting to be your rescue boat in case of emergency. However, there comes a point where having money sitting idly in a bank account becomes unproductive. So, investors are keen to place these funds into longer-term investments that would enable them to keep their money working for them.

It should be noted that long-term investing is not for everyone. In particular, it can be a great option for you if you have money that you are not looking to use any time soon. This is why the safest long-term investment is bonds. When you buy bonds, for example, 6-month or one-year bonds, you are putting your money in a safe spot. While the returns may not blow your mind, you know your money is both safe and generating a return.

That's a lot better than keeping under your mattress.

Advantages of Long-Term Investing

The upside to long-term investing boils down to the following three reasons:

1. **Potential for profit is substantial**

As stated earlier, position investors set themselves up for considerable gains. When playing their cards right, they can cash in trend reversals, market swings, and the changes in investors' psyche. This is why the profit which can be made on a single deal can be far more substantial than the profits made through high-frequency trading. In fact, traders look at day trading as a means of keeping the lights on while looking to position investing as a means of getting rich.

2. **It's less risky**

When you invest in the right instruments, such as government bonds, the potential for risk is a lot lower. In the case of bonds, the only way you could lose your money is if the government went belly up. Unless you buy bonds from not-so-reputable countries, your money will be safe. This is why long-term investing can be a lot less risky when compared to being fully invested in stocks.

3. It's less time consuming

Long-term investing requires a great deal of upfront research. But once you have completed the research needed to take your positions, then you can lay back and simply keep track of the situation. This means that you can devote your attention to other investments or other types of trading, such as day and/or swing trading. In fact, seasoned vets engage in all three types of trading. Naturally, that all depends on the overall amount of time you can devote to trading in addition to the investment capital you have on hand.

Drawbacks of Long-Term Investing

When it comes to long-term investing, there are also drawbacks that need to be considered.

1. Much more capital is needed

This is the biggest issue with position trading. Day traders can make a go start with very little money as they are consistently using the same capital over and over. This is why high-frequency traders can double their money in a short period of time. In long-term investing, much more capital is needed because money is parked for a much longer time period. This is especially true if you are looking to make a huge deal. Position investors generally invest thousands of dollars per trade as opposed to a couple of hundred that day traders may allocate. While there is no requisite number, a good ballpark for position trading is to be at least in the six-figure range. Naturally, you will not invest all of it in a single deal; you will need this kind of money to ensure you make it big.

2. Time is a huge factor

Time is the biggest issue when it comes to long-term investing. If you are in need of making quick profits, then this approach is not for you. Ideally, you would allocate money into long-term investments that you don't actually need. Now, that might sound funny at the moment. But the fact of the matter is that high-level investors reach a point in which they have money they don't need. So, these funds are ideal for long-term investing.

3. A good deal of experience is needed

The reason why long-term investing is not recommended to novice investors is due to the fact that investors need to be cognizant of what the market may or may not do. This type of instinct can only be sharpened with time and experience. As a result, novice investors may find it very difficult to truly gauge what the markets will do over an extended period of time.

Stocks to Hold for Long-Term

This is a question for the ages. Stocks to hold on to for the long haul are the so-called "blue chip" stocks. These are proven winners which have a solid track record. They are also usually very expensive. Nevertheless, when you are able to buy into them, you will find that the return on them is far greater than the bulk of the market.

If you find it unaffordable at this point to get into blue-chip stocks, you might consider an index fund. These funds can be invested specifically in blue-chip companies. Consequently, you don't need to actually own any stock. Rather, you are getting exposure to these stocks. While the returns might be lower than if you actually traded the stocks themselves, you would still be getting solid returns, particularly if you are planning on investing money that you don't need right away.

Now, if you are able to afford individual shares of these companies, you can buy up as many as you can and hold on to them, especially during market downturns. Since investors generally panic, they will try to buy up as many of the best stocks. This is where you cash in. In fact, if you can anticipate a market downturn well ahead of time, you can buy up blue-chip stocks at current market prices and then flip them to hungry investors when the downturn occurs.

Chapter 2: Fundamentals of Position Trading

When it comes to position trading, there are a series of elements that comprise its fundamentals. As a position investor, you need to be aware of these. Otherwise, you run the risk of missing out on the underlying principles that will ensure that you make the most of your investment capital.

In this chapter, we are going to take a look at these fundamentals and what you need to do in order to capitalize on them. By the end of this chapter, you'll be able to determine if position trading is right for you. At the very least, you will determine if it is something you want to work your way up to. After all, you can juggle all three types of investment approaches discussed in this book.

Additionally, It's critical that you are totally familiar with the basic components of position trading. That way, you can begin to frame your mindset in both short-term and long-term visions. That way, you can make the most of your skills and experience. At the end of the day, the only limitation you will find is your investment capital.

Use of Technical Analysis and Fundamental Analysis in Position Trading

It goes without saying that technical analysis is absolutely critical in position trading. Without it, you really have no way of knowing what an individual stock may or may not. Moreover, you have no way of knowing what the market, as a whole, stands to do. This is why technical analysis must become your guiding beacon.

Beyond the cold numbers in terms of stock quotes, technical analysis allows you to gain insight into historical data on individual stocks. This is important to note as historical data can help you backtest your assumptions. Likewise, backtesting can also help you disprove claims made by analysts or experts.

As for fundamental analysis, the influence that political, social, and cultural factors can exert over the markets in a longer period of time can be quite considerable. This is why position traders do their best to keep tabs the events around them.

As a general rule of thumb, please keep an eye on economic indicators. Figures on employment, payrolls, consumer confidence, GDP, and sales reports, in addition to corporate earnings, are all indicators that will help you gain a sense of what investors are looking to do, both in the short and long term.

Lastly, if you have the chance to talk to other investors, do so. In this regard, we're talking about regular investors who work for themselves or have perhaps hired professional money managers. It's always great to talk shop and exchange notes. Who knows that information you might be able to dig up? Plus, getting a sense of what other investors are thinking is a great way to gauge your strategy. This will allow you to assess your own strategy in such a way that you can fine-tune any aspects which you may have overlooked.

Long-Term Investment Instruments

Once you have determined that long-term investing works for you, it's important to figure out where to allocate your money. In this regard, it's worth looking into the various types of instruments in which you can place your money. We will begin by talking about the safest and moving on to the riskiest.

The safest long-term investment is government bonds. There is no question about it. Government bonds, particularly issued by stable countries, can provide you with the assurance you need. And while the returns aren't always mind-blowing, bonds pay more than the average investment account.

As for corporate bonds, these are highly risky. Even with blue-chip companies, there is no assurance that they will endure into the long-term. There have been many cases in which industry leaders go belly-up. So, corporate bonds always have a higher risk than government bonds. However, corporate bonds do pay a higher yield. Hence, it's a question of assessing just how risk the corporation truly is.

Then, index and mutual funds are a great way of parking your money in a long-term passive investment. They produce a higher yield than bonds. Additionally, they offer the opportunity for diversification. Mutual and index funds are also good if you want to day trade while setting some additional money aside for other purposes. You could save up money for a down payment on a house by stashing in an index fund. You would just have to negotiate the term so that you can access it reasonably quickly.

You can also make long-term investments by holding actual stock. It should be noted that index funds don't represent ownership of any kind of stock. So, when you buy real shares of a company, you are exposing yourself to the performance of that particular firm. This is why we encourage investors to look for blue-chip companies as much as possible. However, if you are keen on taking on money risk, you can look at lower-tier companies which have a good upside. These companies may provide solid returns, especially if they are poised to make a significant jump in their respective market.

Lastly, there are ETFs. ETFs are risky because their performance is tied to an asset such as a commodity. As a result, there is no real way you can guarantee their performance. In fact, you may be overwhelmed by the returns an ETF can generate while other times, it may fall flat. This is why you need to be cognizant of the underlying asset in the ETF and how you can profit from it. Most investors who choose to allocate their funds into ETFs choose highly liquid assets such as oil or currencies.

Please note that there is the derivatives market. These types of instruments, such as mortgage-backed securities, are highly risky and generally highly leveraged. Please refrain from investing in these instruments unless you are totally aware of their implications. Since they can be quite complex, we recommend that you do your due diligence on these before investing.

Identifying Long-Term Trend

Long-term trend can be tricky to spot. The reason for this is that you need to look at the right timeframe in order to properly assess a trend. This is why position investors like to look at the various types of moving average. You can start with the 10-day moving average and try to spot a trend. Generally, you should be able to see one even at this point. However, don't be surprised if you only manage to see a sideways trend. At the 10-day mark, this is quite normal.

Then, the next step is to look at the 20-day moving average. At this point, you should be able to clearly see a trend. It might still look sideways, but this timeframe should allow you to get a good sense of where the long-term direction is heading.

The next two timeframes are crucial is spotting a long-term trend. The 50-day moving average is a great indicator of where prices sit. However, then compared to the 200-day moving average, you can really see if there is confirmation of trend, or if there is a trend reversal.

To do this, you need to use the MACD as a means of confirming continuation or reversal. The easiest way to spot a trend reversal is when the 50-day moving average cross over the 200-day moving average. Now, you might see the 10-day and 20-day moving averages intersect, but there are only short-term movements. They may have very little bearing on the long-term trend. That's why position investors pay very close attention to the 50 and 200-day moving averages. As long as these two moving averages do not cross over, then you have a continuation of trend.

Once the 50-day and 200-day moving average have crossed over, then you may find divergence in these prices. In some cases, both moving averages may run parallel to one another. In other cases, you may have a very clear divergence. When these two lines run relatively parallel to one another, it means that investors aren't totally sure of which direction they will head. However, if you see a clear divergence, then you know where investors are heading.

To further cement your analysis, check out the candlesticks. These will confirm the direction in which prices are heading. If you happen to spot short candlesticks, you are seeing unsure investors. However, long candlesticks are a good indication that investors know where they want to go.

Ignoring Short-Term Gains

Since position trading is all about keeping tabs on what's going on regularly, you might find that there are significant fluctuations on a day to day basis. In fact, you might be really encouraged to see spikes in price, such as in a head and shoulders pattern. But, please be advised that these spikes may only be indicative of short-term movements.

You see, investors who are playing the short-term game generally get caught up in the hype that surrounds stocks. After all, they are looking to ride the waves and make short-term windfall profits. As a position investor, you are not looking at the short-term gains. In fact, you could both day and position trade a stock, but that shouldn't cloud your judgment as to the overall price action.

Unless you see a massive gain in a long-term position, it's best to resist the temptation of cashing out early. The problem with doing this is that once a stock reaches a certain price point, you won't be able to get into at a lower price point unless you waited for it to come back down. However, there is no telling when that may happen. So, if you get into a stock at a very low price point, it's best to hold on to it as long as it takes to reach your desired price point.

For instance, you pick up a stock at $5 a share. You anticipate it will hit $20 in roughly eight weeks' time. By week five, it spikes from $7 to $15. At this point, you are tempted to sell and re-enter the position. Sure, you'll make a tidy profit, but then you won't be able to get into the position at the same $5 price point. You might end up getting in at $14 or $15. At this point, you might feel that you'll still make a profit when it hits $20.

But what if it doesn't?

This is where you would be taking unnecessary risk. Unless the stock suddenly jumped to $25 after five weeks, it's best to hold on to it until it reaches your desired price point.

Spotting Long-Term Breakouts

Long-term breakouts depend on both technical analysis and instinct. There are times when companies get stuck at a certain share price because they are unable to improve their sales or generate the hype needed to get investors to take a chance on them. Then, there are companies that are perennial underachievers. But, there are companies that poised to breakout. These are the companies that have great products in the pipeline or are highly disruptive in their respective field. These can also be up and coming stars that have a product or technology that hasn't been perfect yet.

These companies are the ones that you want to get into in the early going. They may have shares trading at ridiculously low prices. So, they may be worth taking a flyer on. If they really do take off, then you will make a killing on their stock once it soars. There is the possibility that such companies never deliver on their promise. In which case, you may have to make an assessment on whether they are worth holding on to or not.

As for blue-chip companies, the technical data will reveal everything you really need to know. Since we're are talking about well-established companies, there really isn't much guesswork. Still, it could be that they provide you with innovations that could lead to a long-term breakout. This is why conducting thorough research may lead you to uncover an unexpected boost. So do keep this in mind when looking into established market leaders.

Chapter 3: Building Wealth Through Position

Trading

Throughout this book, we've mentioned how day trading is intended to keep the lights on. In other words, day trading is meant to be a trading approach that can produce enough profits to help you make the most of your finances by supplementing your income. In fact, day trading is not meant to replace your day job, especially if you earn a decent wage.

However, when you put day and swing trading, you may be able to replace your regular wage and dedicate your time and attention to trading as a full-time career. Plenty of folks have done it. So, it's definitely a question of making sense of the various options at your disposal.

With that in mind, you can use position trading to actually build wealth. By "building wealth," we mean making the most of your abilities and skills to accumulate money, among other assets. You see, when you hold stock of valuable companies, you know that you are going to be in a good position no matter what the market is like. While other investors are getting wiped out by a market downturn, you are in a position to stay afloat.

So, let's take a look at three ways in which position trading can help you build wealth.

Protection Against Shifts in the Market

When you are invested mainly in blue-chip stocks or safer assets such as bonds, short-term shifts should not affect you. Unless there was a seismic shift in the market, you would find that holding these assets will protect the bulk of your wealth in the long-term. Plus, blue-chips and bonds are highly liquid. This means that if you ever needed money in a pinch, you could easily sell them to raise cash. That's why you will find that most investors like to have an allocation to these assets. Recommended allocations range from 10% to 20% bonds (depending on prevailing market conditions) and somewhere around a 25% allocation for blue-chips.

In addition, some investors like to have exposure to commodities such as oil or gold. You can do this by means of ETFs. Generally speaking, 5% to 10% allocation to commodities works rather well. So, do take the time to consider what this asset class can do for you.

Diversification Against Risk

Diversification is the ultimate hedge against risk. This is why you need to make sure that you have your portfolio spread out across the various asset classes we have discussed. Investors who dabble in all three levels of trading like to maintain the bulk of their assets in long-term investments. These investors like to leave about a quarter of their investment capital allocated specifically to day and swing trading. Please note that you don't need to allocate significant funds toward day trading since you don't need a great deal of investment capital to make in short-term, high-frequency trading.

Additionally, adjusting your allocation according to current market conditions is a must. You cannot expect to build wealth by setting your investments on autopilot. This is a passive investment approach that would require you to hire a professional money manager. If you are keen on setting your investments on autopilot, then you might want to consider buying into index funds and ETFs that don't require you to play an active role. That way, you can use your time to research other types of instruments, which could yield positive results for you.

Maintaining a Balanced Portfolio

A balanced portfolio depends on what you are looking to achieve. Some investors start out with a much larger capital. So, their main goal is to preserve their wealth over the long haul. Other investors start out with very little capital. As such, they are looking to build their way up.

Based on your starting point, you can afford to be more or less aggressive. On the whole, smaller investors tend to be much more aggressive as they have a lot more ground to make up. This is why day trading is always the best place to start for smaller investors.

Nevertheless, maintaining a balanced portfolio essentially depends on current market conditions. For instance, when the stock market is booming, it makes sense to have a larger allocation to stocks. By the same token, when the stock market is going through a bear market, it's best to reduce your overall exposure to non-blue-chip stocks.

When the stock market is booming, investors like to be aggressive. This implies taking a chance on startups and new IPOs. When things are going well, high-level investors tend to pull out of index funds and ETFs and go straight into direct stock ownership. You stand to make more money by flipping stock itself since there is any number of investors looking to get in.

In contrast, high-level investors seek shelter in other types of investments, like gold and bonds, when the market is going through a downturn. Whenever you are investing in a bear market, you need to put your money into highly liquid asset classes (FOREX counts in this category, too) so that you can liquidate them in a short timeframe. Please bear in mind that cash is king in a bear market. This is why investors like to have long-term but liquid assets. Instruments like 401(k)s and mutual funds won't help you weather the storm. With these instruments, the only real choice you have is to wait for the storm to pass.

When looking at long-term investing, consider how important it is to preserve wealth. It's one thing to build wealth, but it's another entirely different thing to preserve it. This is why you need to focus on what it takes to keep the money you have worked hard to make. At the end of the day, your ability to preserve your wealth is something that you can pass down from generation to generation. This is why you need to think about what it means to be a successful investor today and into the future.

PART II

Chapter 1: Understanding the Fundamentals of Swing Trading

When it comes to investing, there are other approaches that you can use to your benefit. In this regard, swing trading is another approach that you can consider. Generally speaking, swing trading can offer you a longer-term approach as compared to day trading.

Swing trading can be easily defined as holding open positions for longer than a single trading day. This is done in hopes of capturing the "swings" in the market. As such, you are looking to cash in on price movements, which can lead to profits. The main difference lies in the fact that you are willing to keep your positions open for several days, but usually no longer than a trading week.

It's important to note that periods longer than a week usually require a good deal of study and research, particularly if you are investing in a volatile market. Please keep in mind that swing trading is highly speculative. So, you are attempting to see the future in hopes of translating that into profits. Nevertheless, swing trading can offer you a certain set of advantages that the day trading philosophy can't. By engaging in swing trading, you can open up the door to another set of possibilities.

In this chapter, we are going to explore the fundamentals of swing trading and how you can use it to your advantage. Best of all, you will be able to make the most of your study and research in finding the gems that can provide you with great returns.

The Difference Between Swing Trading and Day Trading

As mentioned earlier, the difference between day trading and swing trading is the length of time in which open positions are held. But the differences don't just stop there. When you are looking toward a longer timeframe, you are also looking toward a longer-term approach. This means that you aren't out to make some quick returns (that's generally the main focus of day trading). Rather, you are looking at the bigger picture.

When you start looking at the bigger picture, you are looking at situations in which you believe things will or won't happen. For instance, you are tracking a specific stock that you feel has the potential to grow. However, it isn't clear when it will happen. So, you can choose to hold on to your position for a few days in order to wait for the right time.

As you can see, swing trading is highly speculative because you are banking on something happening, which you may be sure it will happen, but you just don't know when. This is the speculative nature of this type of investment approach.

Those investors who deal in swing trading need to learn to roll with the punches. This means that it's quite likely that prices may fall before they hit the heights you expect. As a result, you can't let your emotions get the better of you. If you see that prices are suddenly falling, you may have to resist the temptation to pull the plug. Unlike day trading, you need to ride out the storm in a reasonable manner. With swing trading, you need to be reasonably sure that the stock will come back despite any short-term drama. This is why you cannot allow your emotions, namely fear, to get in the way of your overall decisions.

Advantages of Swing Trading

When it comes to the good side of swing trading, there are clear advantages. First of all, swing trading allows you to have a lot more flexibility when it comes to setting up your strategy. Mainly, it enables you to look for hidden gems, the kind that doesn't necessarily pop up in the short-term. Rather, you can look for companies that may be undervalued but look to pop back up within a reasonable time period. For instance, you are looking at tech stocks. One such company has recently announced that they will be unveiling a new product. So, you decide to pick up some of their stock days ahead of the unveiling. What you are shooting for is a leap in stock prices as a result of the buzz created by the new product launch. However, if you wait until the actual announcement, then you'll miss the upswing.

Also, you can plan for overnight moves. For example, you spot a company's stock falling at the end of the trading day. So, you decide to swoop in and capitalize on this uncharacteristic drop in price. You hold the position open overnight and plan on selling at the open of the next trading day. Then, when traders are looking to open their positions for the new trading day, you can sell at a higher price thanks to the increased trading activity.

Additionally, swing trading is great for times in which there is increased volatility, that is, significant swings in price action. Since prices don't seem very stable, for example, due to uncertain economic conditions, you can choose to hold on to positions for a bit longer in hopes of catching a sudden surge in the price of an asset. On the contrary, if you are trading within a very predictable and stable environment, you might be better off with short-term trades.

Please bear in mind that swing trading requires patience and careful study. If you are not patient nor keen on studying companies and markets in greater detail, then swing trading may not be for you. After all, it can be nerve-wracking to have positions open when prices are sinking. Since swing trading is so speculative, all you can hope for is that the data you analyzed is right. Of course, there will come a time when you may have to pull the plug. If that should occur, then it's just a matter of licking your wounds and moving on.

Characteristics of a Swing Trader

Earlier, we mentioned that a swing trader needs to be patient. Patience is always the key to long-term investing. You need to be focused on the bigger picture. If you let short-term data get in the way of your vision, you will freak out every time you see the price of your chose stock falling. Since there is an ebb and flow to all stock prices, you need to be honed in on the overall trend of a stock's price. This is the essence of long-term investing.

Swing traders also need to be very detail-oriented. This means that you need to be cognizant of what the data and the financials are telling you about a company.

If the financials reveal that the company is doing well, but has come under fire recently due to a bad economy, then you may be confident that the company will bounce back. By the same token, it may be that all stocks are getting crushed by a bad economy, political decisions, or investor skepticism. As such, you are ready to pounce on cheap stocks and prepared to sell when they rebound. A classic example of this occurs during elections. Investors hold their breath until there is a winner. In the meantime, you can scoop up some undervalued stocks hoping to catch the rebound once the election is over.

In addition, swing traders need to be very objective. Often, you hear gurus and experts talking about what they expect will happen with the market or a particular stock. Yet, you see that the numbers are telling a different story. This means that you need to be able to filter out the noise. You need to focus on the data and see if the experts are right or if they are full of hot air. The numbers don't lie. So, you need to trust the numbers as far as you can.

But being objective does not mean that you should ignore your gut. As you develop your skills and sharpen your instincts, you'll be able to follow hunches. Now, this doesn't mean rolling the dice on a feeling. What it means is that a hunch can be proven by the data. Often, hunches can go against what experts are recommending. Your instincts can also save you from disaster. It could very well be that gurus are screaming for you to buy when you should be selling. So, always take expert advice with a grain of salt. Your instincts are there to help you navigate turbulent water.

Lastly, swing traders are built on experience. This is why most financial experts recommend novice investors to start off with day trading, that is a short-term approach, before moving on to swing trading. As you gain more experience, you'll become familiar with the shifts in the market. As you sharpen your vision, you'll be able to recognize these shifts, thereby allowing you to make the right moves ahead of time. When you are eventually able to combine sound technical and quantitative analysis with instincts and experience, there is no telling how well you can do. The sky literally is the limit.

Conducting Research as a Swing Trader

Research is part of any successful trader's strategy. Without it, there is no way that you can reasonably ascertain what future price action might look like. As such, you need to be focused on what you can expect when engaging in swing trading.

For starters, studying trend is a vital part of swing trading. For example, you are tracking a company. You see that it has a bearish trend. As such, you are looking to track a potential reversal, that is, from bearish to bullish. So, you are keen on buying at the lowest possible point right before the trend reverses and becomes bullish. When you buy at the lowest possible point, you can maximize your gains. However, it might take several days for the price to reach the low point. Once the price hits the lowest mark, you jump in. Then, it may take several more days before the price hits the ceiling and bounces back down. Naturally, you would be keen to sell at the highest possible point before the next trend reversal.

This is why you need to be patient when engaging in swing trading. This is all possible thanks to your dedicated research.

But beyond technical analysis, there is also fundamental analysis. Fundamental analysis is the study of factors that are outside of quantitative tools such as price, trading volume, and so on. With fundamental analysis, you are studying socio-economic, political, and even cultural factors that may influence stock prices. For instance, retailers tend to post big gains during specific shopping seasons. Consequently, investors may choose to get in on retail stocks right before sales figures are posted following Christmas, Black Friday, and so on.

Also, conducting specific research on a company's board, market share, and even their tax returns are all important when you are looking to make long-term investment decisions. In fact, some companies may be down in the dumps but poised for a turnaround following changes in management and so on. These are factors that you can uncover by doing careful research on their management practices and business decisions.

Thus, research is vitally important when it comes to being a successful swing trader.

Benefits and Drawbacks of Swing Trading

With swing trading, you can expect a series of benefits and drawbacks. Let's take a look at them so you can have a good idea of what to expect as part of your trading endeavors.

Benefits

Here are three major benefits you can expect from swing trading:

1. **Flexibility**. Swing trading gives you the flexibility to place trades and lets them sit as the situation unfolds. This is something you can't do with day trading as you need to be on top of every trade while it's open. Since you may be expecting to keep positions open for several days, all you need to do is keep tabs on your positions while you conduct further research.

2. **Bigger gains**. When you play the swings in price action, you have the potential to make bigger gains. This means that you may go from earning pennies on each trade to earning hundreds, if not thousands of dollars on a single trade. Since you are holding out longer in an open position, this can expand the potential for bigger gains.

3. **Less trading activity.** In swing trading, you are poised to make more profits per trade. So, you need to make fewer trades. With day trading, you need to make lots more trades to make the amount of profits you would from a single one. In the end, you have the opportunity to do far more with less. In fact, you may not even have to make a single trade on a daily basis. You would only have to make trades when the situation calls for it.

Drawbacks

Now, let's take a look at three major drawbacks that come with swing trading:

1. **Increased exposure to risk.** Having open positions for longer time periods exposes you to increased risk. The reason for this is that any number of unforeseen factors can take place. This makes you more vulnerable to price swings that can make your trade go south. As a result, you need to be vigilant about the price action. While this doesn't require you to watch your positions like a hawk, you do need to stay on top of things. You can't simply expect to set everything on autopilot.

2. **More investment capital is needed.** Since you have positions open for much longer, you need to increase your position size. Smaller amounts of capital are useful when you engage in high-frequency trading as you are investing the same amount over and over again. With long-term investing, you need more investment capital to make more significant leaps. This is why day traders start off small, then build up their investment capital. This means going from a few hundred dollars to a few thousand.

3. **Losses are magnified.** Just like profits are magnified by significant swings in price action, losses are also magnified. So, if a trade goes south, and increased position size can cause you to see your losses increase. That's why keeping an eye on your open

positions is a great way of keeping your investments safe. If something unexpected happens, you can pull the plug in time. Otherwise, you may be too late.

Please take the time to consider the benefits and drawbacks of swing trading. If you feel that this could be a good fit for you, then by all means, consider taking part in this approach. Still, it's recommended to start off with short-term investing before working your way up.

Swing Trading Assets

Swing trading does not only apply to stocks. There are other types of assets that you can trade using the swing trading approach. So, let's take a look at them.

Swing trading commodities

When you swing trade stocks, you are basically at the mercy of how well the company performs. Then, you are banking on the psychological impression that investors receive based on a company's performance.

When you consider entering the commodities market, you can also cash in on some interesting gains. Commodities are all physical goods that are traded, such as oil, metals, and agricultural products, among others. When you dabble in commodities, you are looking at what the market can do based on their expectations of goods.

Let's consider oil. When you trade oil, price action may seem rather stagnant in the short-term. Price may only fluctuate a few pennies throughout a trading session. But when you magnify this price action over days or even weeks, you can make some significant gains. Therefore, it's worth looking into commodities. You can enter this market by purchasing contracts. These contracts are essentially a promise to of future delivery. These can be quite profitable, especially if the market suddenly turns on a dime.

Swing trading FOREX

When you swing trade FOREX, you are banking on longer-term swings in price action. This can work out very well for you if you believe that one currency may fall in price sharply, or if you believe it will bounce back. These swings are quite significant, especially when there is an uncertain landscape in a county.

For instance, if there is political unrest in a country, investors may begin dumping that country's currency. You can then pick it up on the cheap as you expect the situation to be solved. Then, when the country's political situation is stable once again, you can sell at a higher gain.

In this example, you are engaging in a highly speculative deal. As such, there is a great chance of the deal not working out. This is why swing trading FOREX is not for the faint of heart. In fact, it is for investors who are experienced and know what they are doing. Those who do know their stuff can make massive gains.

Swing trading options

Options can be quite profitable if you hold on to them for a certain amount of time. Mainly, they can provide you with good gains if there are significant fluctuations in prices. These fluctuations may leave investors looking to purchase options that can provide them with a bit more certainty in the midst of an uncertain period. If you are holding these options, you can make some good money.

Swing trading options requires you to become more familiar with the way they work. Please note that options lose value the longer you hold them. Nevertheless, they are valuable in times when price action is less predictable. This means that if you can get in on options when things are stable, you can really clean up when prices suddenly turn. This is possible only if you are keen on seeing where trends are going. If you can spot movements that other investors might not have seen, then you know you can truly make it big.

One the whole, swing trading is a great way for you to spread your wings once you have gained a certain level of proficiency in day trading. So, definitely check it out after you feel totally comfortable with day trading.

Chapter 2: Essentials of Swing Trading

Using technical analysis to your advantage when engaging in swing trading is a must. When you are able to use the quantitative data available to you for the purpose of analyzing potential moves down the road, you will be able to play the long-term game. As a result, this can help you to plan out broader strategies based on the outlook for the market.

In a manner of speaking, swing traders need to get their crystal ball out to identify what may happen in the future. The good news is that you don't need to be psychic to figure this out. All you need is a good set of data and the right tools to come up with a reasonable forecast. The best part is that you don't need an advanced degree in mathematics or finance. All you need is to know where to look.

In this regard, successful trades are all need to stay on top of the data that comes in over the various news services available to them. In fact, full-service brokerage accounts come with specialized information and data services. They publish alerts and other types of notification on breaking news. This makes staying up to date quite straightforward.

In this chapter, we are going to look at the various technical analysis tools which you can use as part of swing trading. These tools are aimed at providing you with the foresight you need to plan trades that go beyond the usual one-day timeframe.

In fact, many of these tools will help you set up your trades in such a way that you can go beyond the typical swing trading parameters. This is important to note, as you will have the chance to set yourself up for even longer-term investing opportunities.

Technical Analysis Tools Used in Swing Trading

As we have stated throughout this book, successful traders need to use quantitative analysis tools to help them make objective decisions. And while we have established that trusting your instincts is a must for good traders, the fact is that you cannot expect to be successful by making subjective decisions. In addition, having solid numerical data can help you take the emotion out of investment decisions. The cold, hard numbers can help you confirm a hunch or dismiss it.

With that in mind, it's important for you to build on the technical analysis tools which we described in the previous chapter. This will allow you to expand your knowledge and understanding of the trend in the market, that is the direction in which it is heading, to a broader timeframe.

As such, analyzing markets as part of swing trading is more about understanding the longer-term trend as opposed to the short-term fluctuations. As you look at the broader picture, you'll see that you can use short-term investing to make quick profits, and thereby build up your earnings, while you can use long-term investing to make significant trades and thereby hit a home run.

The Use of Charts and Graphs

At this point, charts and graphs are essential to keeping track of the information you will be analyzing. Virtually all information services provide you with access to information presented in a visual format. You need to see the information in this manner. Otherwise, it is practically impossible to made heads or tails of it.

The difference then lies in the timeframes that you are permitted to see. Free information services provide you with very detailed information about stocks, commodities, or any other asset you are tracking. The catch is that the information is not in real-time. The information you see is often on a delay. The delay could be slight, say a few minutes, or even longer, such as a few hours. However, even a few minutes can make the difference between making money and just falling flat.

Think about it this way:

If you are late to a birthday party, you can't just burst in singing "Happy Birthday" when everyone has already started eating the cake.

The same goes for trading.

This is why you need real-time data. By having access to the current numbers, you can make a wise assessment of the situation now, and see if the trend that you have been tracking looks to hold up or perhaps change.

Now, it should be said that it is possible for you to make very wise decisions in swing trading even if you don't have real-time data. In fact, real-time data is essential for day traders. However, swing traders can get away with longer timeframes.

Why?

Because you are looking at the bigger picture. You are not looking to make a quick buck. However, since the devil is in the details, real-time data allows you to see the way investors are gauging the specific situation. Therefore, having access to all types of timeframes will give you very detailed snapshots of what's going on.

So, let's dig deeper into the tools that you will be using. You will find that we have already spoken about them. This will make drilling down on them conducive to expanding your horizon.

Use of Moving Average (MACD)

Earlier, we talked about the moving average and how it can allow you to see where the trend in price is heading. The moving average is one of the fundamental tools that investors need to use as it is the clearest indicator of price action. As a result, you cannot disregard this indicator if you want to be successful.

For swing trading purposes, it's important to look at the various timeframes that are commonly studied in trading, that is, the 20-day, 50-day, and 200-day moving average. In particular, we are going to be looking at the 20 and 50-day moving average.

The 20-day average is a great indication of the current trend in a stock's valuation. You could work with the 10-day moving average if you wanted to get a very accurate picture of short-term moves. However, the 10-day moving average does not reflect a broader perspective. This is why the 20-day moving average is a good starting point for swing traders.

Then, the comparison between the 20 and 50-day moving averages will enable you to determine if the trend looks to continue or if it will reverse. A simple way to determine this is by looking at the two trendlines simultaneously. If you find that they are heading in the same direction, then that's all that needs to be said. However, if you find that the lines may intersect at some point, then you might be on the verge of a convergence. If you find that the lines are moving away from one another, then you are looking at a divergence.

Let's start with convergence.

Convergence means that you have the 20-day and 50-day moving averages intersecting at one point. This is the clearest indication that you have of trend reversal. The point at which both of these averages intersect is where you can expect a trend reversal. If you are moving from a bearish trend and spot a reversal to a bullish trend, then this could be your signal to enter the trade. You can then expect the price to go back up until the resistance level (if there is one clearly established). Also, you may spot a bullish trend ending, thereby setting off a reversal into a bullish one; this would be the signal to sell and thus exit the trade.

As you can see, these trend reversals are a great way for you to really clean up.

How so?

By looking at the bigger picture, you can establish the right time when prices will shift. So, you can get in right when the price is about to hit the floor and then ride the wave all the way back up to the top right where it hits the ceiling. Theoretically, these are the highest and lowest possible points. As a result, you can maximize your results.

This approach is great when you are tracking stocks during a period of relatively low volatility, that is, significant fluctuations in price action. Naturally, you can expect to have several ups and downs along the way. But the moving average is what will tell you if you are headed in the right direction.

As for divergence, this is when the 20-day and 50-day moving averages are headed in opposite directions, particularly after a reversal. What you are seeing, in that case, is the market reacting to short-term influence while the long-term outlook is quite different.

Consider this situation:

The government has recently published employment data. The numbers look bad as the economy added fewer jobs than expected. As a result, investors are concerned about the overall health of the economy. Their immediate reaction to the news was to sell off their positions and move money into safer assets.

This is a natural reaction from investors when economic data is not good. However, it is not a reflection of an individual company. So, it could be that its price is sinking in the short-term. In the long-term, though investors feel confident in this company. So, it's a question of the economy weighing the company's stock price more than the company's performance.

This is why you need to take things with a grain of salt. Not all fluctuations are signs of trouble. You just need to be cognizant of what they mean and why they were caused. It could be that short-term, the stock you are looking at has fallen. But the overall, long-term trend looks solid. So, you can reasonably expect the price to come back and reach the heights you are expecting once investors recover from the initial shock of bad economic data.

The study of the moving average and its convergence and divergence is known as the "Moving Average Convergence Divergence" model or MACD. By studying the MACD, you can get a pretty good picture of where prices figure to be headed at some point in the not-too-distant future. Please bear in mind that swing trading is about keeping your eyes within a few days. So, it's always a good idea to compare both short-term and long-term data.

Significant Levels

Since you are analyzing longer-term data, you will find that significant levels may change. This means that you may have broader peaks and troughs. These points can differ significantly when compared to short-term data. In fact, you may find that 10 days' worth of data reveals the price of the stock trading in a narrow range. But when you expand it to 20 or 50 days' worth of data, the floor and ceiling at found at much higher and lower points. This can be due to short-term factors affecting a stock while the overall trend of the stock is holding a given pattern.

Let's take a look at these considerations.

First, let's assume you have a stock trading in a very narrow band over a 10-day period. This is something that should surprise you, especially if the trading volume is low. The reason for this is that investors may be holding out for news (economic data, for instance), or they may be allocating their investment dollars elsewhere. But when you amplify the data set to a longer timeframe, you see that there are larger fluctuations. This indicates that trading activity settled down to a much lower level. If anything, this could be a signal for a potential trend reversal. So, you need to pay attention to the moving average.

Second, you have a rather narrow band in the longer data set while you have significant peaks and troughs in the shorter timeframe. This is typical of short-term factors affecting investors' appreciation of the stock. It could be that there was unfavorable economic data published, the company went through a minor situation or perhaps the overall industry was affected by some sort of shock. This can be picked up by unusual levels of trading activity in the short-term.

If you are keen on combining a short and long-term approach, you can make money off the short-term fluctuations while setting up your positions for longer-term movements such as trend reversals. Generally speaking, seasoned swing traders like to combine both approaches. It's like killing two birds with one stone.

Trend Continuation

Thus far, we have focused quite a bit on trend reversal. The reason for this is that trend reversal is the best point in which you can maximize your profits. However, trend continuation is also a great way for you to make significant gains.

How so?

Consider this situation:

You are tracking the moving average of a given stock. Both the 20 and 50-day moving average seem to be in sync. This is a clear indication of a trend continuation. So, you decide to keep going with a short-term trading strategy as a long-term approach doesn't seem like it would yield greater benefits. Or, you could take both short and long-term positions. The short-term position allows you to make money off the usual fluctuations given the band that the stock is trading in. The long-term position allows you to capitalize on the increasing price of the stock (assuming a bullish trend). However, if you find that the stock is trading in a range but has a bearish trend, it might be best if you held off for a bit longer until you can spot a trend reversal.

Overall, trend continuation is a good thing, especially if you can combine both a long and short-term approach. In the end, you shouldn't be limited by just one approach. The more you combine approaches, the more money you stand to make.

The Head and Shoulders Pattern

This is where trend reversal and continuation get fun. With this pattern, you can spot a potential change in trend, particularly if a stock is trading in a narrow band.

The "head and shoulders" pattern is used to determine if there will be a breakout or a continuation of trend. This pattern can serve investors to determine if prices will stay in the same range or if they are poised for a breakout.

The pattern consists of one spike (which hits on the ceiling), then a large spike (which breaks part the ceiling), and after returning back to the usual range, there is a third spike that reaches the ceiling but not past. So, the first spike is the first should, the large spike is the head, and the third spike is the second shoulder. When you see this pattern, especially if there is a bullish trend, you can expect the price to break out of the range at some point. When it happens depends on the overall direction and tempo of the trend. In some cases, it may take days, while in other cases, it may take weeks.

Also, the reverse is possible. You may have the head and shoulder forming at the bottom of the price action chart. In that case, you can expect the price to go further down. Confirmation of this trend occurs when there is a bearish trend.

With this pattern, watch out for false signals. The most common false signal is the pattern, while there is the opposite trend. For instance, you may believe that a breakout is about the take place. However, a bearish trendline would indicate that this is not the case. The same may occur with a potential breakthrough the floor. This is unlikely, especially if the trend is bullish.

Triple Tops and Triple Bottoms

Triple tops and bottoms are mainly used to confirm significant levels. This pattern consists of three consecutive hits at one point (or very close it the same point) either at the resistance or support level. When this occurs, you can confirm a resistance or support level.

The main difference between the triple tops and bottoms with the head and shoulders pattern is that there are no spikes that breakout of either significant level. This is why it is used to confirm a significant level. When you see the three successive hits (that is three hits on a row), without any hits surpassing the others, then you can safely confirm a resistance or support level.

Further confirmation of the significant level is achieved when you match it with the trendline. So, if you have a triple top alongside a bullish trendline, then you have confirmed a resistance level. If you have a triple bottom with a bearish trendline, you have confirmed a floor.

Also, it is possible to have both triple tops and bottoms in the same data set you are analyzing. When this occurs, you can confirm that the stock is trading in a range. Often, this may also indicate that the range is narrow. Additionally, it is also an indication that investors are undecided and may be waiting for further signals before taking action.

Candlestick Analysis

Candlesticks are rectangular boxes that are oriented vertically. These boxes have a line that shoots from its top and bottom. The box is called the "body," while the lines are called "shadows." The body of a candlestick indicates the opening price of the stock and its closing price. If the body is long, then there is a considerable spread among the opening and closing prices. The shadows indicate the high and low prices. The upper shadow indicates the high price, while the lower shadow indicates the low price.

The prices that are reflected in a candlestick are the measure of price action in a given period. In the case of stocks, it is usually measured on a daily basis. However, lower timeframes may show candlesticks on an hourly basis.

When analytics software shows you moving average information, it will display candlesticks. So, rather than just getting one price quoted, you get four prices in a single candlestick. You can tell how price is doing overall just by visually inspecting the candlesticks. If you see short candlesticks with equally short shadows, then the price is trading in a range. The shorter the candlestick, the narrower the range. If you see long candlesticks with long shadows, then you have a large spread among the various price measurements. This is an indication of increased volatility in the market.

On the whole, candlesticks are a great way for you to visualize what the moving average represents for you in any given situation. So, make sure that you pay close attention to the candlesticks, particularly at the top and bottom of a price action curve. When you see very short candlesticks right the highest or lowest point of a chart, you are receiving a signal that a trend reversal is about to take place.

"Timing" entry and exit points

To "time" entry and exit points in a trade, you can use the MACD. It's a simple, yet very effective way to assess trend reversal. To do this, we will examine divergence. As you begin to recognize this pattern, you'll be able to either confirm continuation of trend, or a possible reversal in short order.

Here is how it works:

- First, take a look at the moving average action. When you see that the price of the stock makes significant swings up or down thereby moving above or below the moving average, you may have a signal.
- Next, look at the trading volume. If trading volume is commensurate to the swing, then you have confirmation. For instance, if the price swings up and momentum also swings up, the you have a signal that price will go up. This could be the moment to time your exit point.
- Also, if the price swings down and you have significant increase in the "sell" side of the trading volume histogram, then you have confirmation of the price falling. This could be your moment to buy or enter a trade.
- Then, look to see if the swings are contrary to the swing in price. If there is a cross over, but the trading volume remains the same, then you have a false signal. Here, the best way to go is to hold your position until you get further confirmation.

The only caveat to this pattern is a series of bursts and dips that appear to be random. In such cases, you may want to anticipate your move. Setting up stops and take-profit points would help you exit the trade while still profiting or before you take a significant hit.

Chapter 3: Risk Management in Swing Trading

One of the most important elements in trading is managing risk. As we have stated throughout this book, risk is an inherent part of trading. We cannot expect to engage in trading without somehow running into it. This is why this chapter is focused on risk and how we can mitigate its potential impact on our trading activity. In addition, we'll be looking at practical ways in which you can keep yourself protected from unexpected events.

Protecting Yourself Against Risk

In swing trading, risk is amplified due to the length in which your positions remain open. This means that you are more vulnerable to unforeseen events in the markets. Nevertheless, there are also ways in which you can avoid getting burned. So, let's take a look at five ways in which you can keep yourself free from danger as much as possible.

1. **Diversification is key**

Diversification is the ultimate antidote to risk. The reason for this lies in the fact that you are not exposing your entire portfolio to a single stock or asset class. The reasoning behind diversification is that by separating your portfolio allocation across various asset classes and stocks, you can offset the losses from one asset with the gains from another. This is important as it will enable you to avoid getting pummeled by a single diminishing asset. If anything, you'll be able to ensure that you recoup any losses rather quickly.

2. Always have a plan

The need for a plan cannot be stressed enough. The main reason for having a plan at all times is that it takes the guesswork out of whatever you are doing. For instance, if you are faced with an unexpected situation, you will know how to react. In fact, when you don't have a plan, you waste a lot of time trying to react. When you have a plan, you won't waste any time. As a result, you can get in front of the situations that you are facing.

3. Never forget to set up stop-loss and take-profit points

When you are trading in general, not just swing trading; it's important to set up a stop-loss point. This point consists of an automatic point at which the system cuts your losses. This is necessary as you may not have time to react to the action going on around you. Consequently, the stop-loss points kick in at the price point you have determined. When this occurs, your position is automatically closed, thereby saving you from disaster. By the same token, a take-profit point is an automatic sell point once you have reached your desire profit. Sure, it might sting if you see that you could have made a larger profit. But, at the end of the day, this will help you keep your expectations in check.

4. It's always best to err on the side of caution

It's great if you are aggressive. However, being too aggressive can be a problem, especially in the early going. Additionally, it's easy to become too aggressive when you are on a roll. If you see that you have put up a consistent winning streak, you might feel compelled to take on more and more risk. This is why it's important to keep risk within reasonable means. Otherwise, you may find yourself opening the door to unwanted situations.

5. **Stick to the 2% rule**

Earlier, we mentioned day traders should keep their individual positions to 1% to 2% of their entire investment portfolio. We encourage the same for swing traders. If you decide to invest anything beyond this allocation, you are opening up the door to trouble. While more experienced traders are willing to go as far as 5%, please note that it's always best to err on the side of caution. Unless you have gained ample experience with an asset class or specific company, anything beyond 2% could prove regretful down the road.

Psychology in Swing Trading

Psychology plays a crucial role in making sound investment decisions. In swing trading, psychology is just as important as it is in day trading. The difference lies in one crucial element: patience. Many investors get into the game hoping they can hit a home run right away. While that's quite possible, please bear in mind that there is no such thing as "beginner's luck" in investing. So, it's important for you to learn how to manage your emotions and your expectations.

If you plan to start out with day trading and work your way up to swing trading, please note that you will be forced to exercise more patience. This means that you won't see the fruits of your investments until several days down the road. This is important as the longer you are able to hold onto your position, the more profit you stand to make.

Another important element in swing trading psychology is ambition. This is why stop-loss and take-profit points are absolutely essential. When you set up these points, it's like flying on autopilot. Now, this is important as you may get caught up in trying to squeeze an extra bit of profit out of a trade. However, the action moves so fast in the stock market that you may not have enough time to react. This is why setting up your points will help keep you safe from getting nailed by unforeseen events.

Lastly, all seasoned traders and investors know that it's best to push back from the table when you're angry. If you engage in "revenge investing," you are really asking for it. Revenge investing consists of upping the ante when you miss on a trade. Let's say that you lose $100 on a deal. So, you might be tempted to place $200 on the next deal. Needless to say, this is not the most effective way. If you lose, shake it off and stick to the plan. If it is clear that the plan is not working, then it would be time to shut things down and revise your strategy.

Fundamental Analysis

Fundamental analysis tends to get overlooked by investors. Fundamental analysis consists of analyzing social, political, and even cultural factors that might influence investors. When you ignore fundamental analysis, you are disregarding important factors that can have a powerful influence on investors' mindsets. A classic example of this happens during an election cycle. The market generally reacts to the poll leader ahead of the election and then to the winner following the election.

Likewise, markets react to economic data like unemployment figures, GDP data, and even the potential of natural disasters.

Think about this situation:

Suppose that a major hurricane is set to slam into the oil refineries located on the Gulf of Mexico. This means that refineries need to shut down production for a couple of days while the storm passes. Investors react to this by buying up as much gasoline supply as they can. The end result of this psychological reaction to a natural disaster is a hike in gas prices.

As you can see, it's quite plausible to have factors that are completely unrelated to quantitative data impact the behavior of investors. So, you need to keep tabs on these factors. Otherwise, you won't be getting the full picture. Keeping up with the latest news is the easiest way for you to ensure that you don't miss anything when it comes to the world around you.

Backtesting Strategies

Backtesting consists of taking historical data and using it to test out your strategy. This approach is very useful in determining whether or not your assumptions are correct. Please bear in mind that focusing your attention solely on the most current data may leave you with a biased outlook. In fact, all successful investors are mindful of historical data. You'll be surprised to see the patterns and trends that you may find when backtesting your strategies.

For example, you are looking at a particular stock that's valued at $10 a share. When you look back at the data, you find that the stock was valued at a much higher price, say, $15 a share. So, you begin to research why this company's stock price fell so much. Here, you learn that the company went through a rough patch because of a management scandal. By now, the company has turned over its management team, and its financials look good. This would be a candidate for swing trading as you are expecting their stock price to rebound in short order.

This example highlights how going back in time may reveal some hidden gems. By the same token, it may reveal hidden lemons that you want to stay away from. For instance, a company's stock price is soaring. But when you look back at its historical data, you determine that it's simply overvalued. So, the best way to go here would day trade it and ride the short-term hype. Since the company is simply overvalued, you feel its best to avoid holding on to it for any considerable timeframe. This is why looking back in time can help you avoid a potential problem down the road.

-

PART III

Chapter 1: Understanding the Fundamentals of Day Trading

As mentioned in the introduction, day trading is a short-term investment approach. This approach is based mainly on stocks. As such, day traders trade stocks of publicly-traded companies in the United States. While it is possible to trade the stock of international companies, they would have to be listed for public trading in the United States. So, for the purpose of this book, we are going to be focusing on the United States stock market.

Traditionally, the only way an average person could invest in the stock market was through a brokerage firm. This meant that the average investor had to go to their local bank or investment firm to open up a brokerage account. From there, a stockbroker or professional money manager would handle their investment capital.

This is still done today. The difference is that technology has now enabled us to cut out the middleman, that is, we no longer need to take a trip down to a bank or investment firm to open up an investment account. In fact, you can do this now from the comfort of your home. Thanks to the internet, there is no need to seek out the services of professional stockbrokers and money managers.

It should be noted that when you choose to make your own investment decisions, you need to be cognizant of what you are doing. Sure, it may seem like it's just a matter of buying and selling stocks, but there's more to it than that. The fact of the matter is you need to be aware of how the process works.

That's why we're here!

As such, folks who wish to invest their money themselves can become a "day trader." This term refers to those investors who open and close their positions within the same trading day. This means that you can zero stocks when you start your trading day, buy up a bunch of stocks, and then sell everything off before you close shop for the day.

This is the classic definition.

There is an expanded definition that considers leaving open positions overnight. However, we will not encourage you to do so in this book as leaving positions open overnight can be quite dangerous, particularly due to the increase in trading volume that occurs at the beginning of each trading day.

The reason why day trading exists is because trading occurs from Monday to Friday from 9 am to 4 pm. This is when stock exchanges are open. A stock exchange is the physical place in which trading takes place. In the olden days, this was the trading floor that is commonly featured in films. Nowadays, the building still exists, and it still houses offices. However, most of the trading is done by computers. The most famous stock exchange is the New York Stock Exchange located on Wall Street. Yet, it is not the only one. There are others in Chicago, Philadelphia, and Miami.

At this point, it should be noted that we are not endorsing day trading as a full-time job. While you could certainly do it, it is not advisable to quit your day job and become a full-time day trader until you have the experience and the confidence needed to replace your current income source. Nevertheless, when you do build up the skills and experience, you can make a lot more money trading than working at any job (unless it was a very high-paying job).

Characteristics of a Day Trader

There is no need to have special skills or training to become a day trader. Sure, it would help if you had a degree in finance or economics, but there is nothing that would keep you from becoming a successful day trader is you didn't have a degree in these areas.

In fact, the most successful day traders are the folks that are able to understand the fundamentals of the markets and how to manage the trading platform. Beyond that, all you really need is common sense. Unfortunately, this isn't something that is taught in graduate programs. Most professionals with advanced degrees get caught up in complex models that don't always reflect the fundamentals of the markets.

This is where anyone with common sense can really flourish. When you understand how the market works, you won't have to figure out any complex models and systems. Everything you need to know is laid out for you. All you need to do is make sense of it all.

Nevertheless, there are some personal qualities that day traders need to have. Firstly, all good traders need to be patient. Being "trigger happy" is not a good way to make money when trading. Secondly, traders should be cautious. This means that you need to study your strategy before putting it into practice. The more you study, the easier it will be to avoid making big mistakes. Thirdly, successful traders are proactive. This means that they are able to anticipate movements in the market before they happen. This is a quality that is developed over time. But when this instinct is fully sharpened, it can lead to significant profits well before the majority of investors wake up and smell the coffee.

So, do take the time to ponder these characteristics. By embracing them, you will be giving yourself the best chance to be successful.

Day Trading as a Full-Time Career

Earlier, we mentioned that while it is not advisable to quit your day job to pursue day trading full time, it is entirely possible to make a career out of it. In fact, there are plenty of stories out there of folks who have made this transition.

Generally speaking, it is perfectly possible to do so. However, this depends on your ability to learn the ropes effectively and make consistent returns. Since day trading is based on the stock market and its fluctuations, consistent returns aren't always guaranteed. This is why the learning curve in trading can be steep at times. Nevertheless, if you are able to consistently deliver on the results that you need to finance your lifestyle, you could certainly make a career out of it.

Most folks start out trading in their free time. As they gain momentum, they devote more and more time to it. Eventually, they are able to supplement their income quite well. This gives them the flexibility to work less hours at their regular job or are transitioning into a full-time investing career. The important thing to keep in mind here is that making day trading a full-time career eventually becomes a job of its own. Your challenge would be to manage your time so that you can make money while enjoying the flexibility that comes with trading.

The Difference Between Day, Swing, and Position Trading

By definition, day trading is a short-term investment approach. As stated earlier, day trading involves opening and closing positions within the same trading day. On the surface, this seems like you won't have too much time to reap the rewards of your investments. However, please be assured that there is money to be made in such a short time period. As a matter of fact, most of the action happens at the beginning and end of the trading day.

This is why we mentioned that it could be dangerous to leave positions open overnight. You see, at the start of the trading day, investors place their first trades before the stock exchanges open. This allows them to capitalize on the previous day's closing price. Then, when the market opens, a flood of orders goes through the door. This is why you see investors placing their orders within the first two hours following the open of the market. After those first two hours, the trading volume reduces significantly. It is said that you should trade between 11 am and 2 pm as there isn't much action going on during that time. While that is certainly true, if you are looking to make a quick buck, the truth is there is always money to be made at any time.

In contrast, swing trading enables investors to keep positions open for multiple days but never longer than a full week. So, this means that you could open up your positions on Monday morning and close them up on Friday afternoon. With swing trading, you are giving yourself a chance to cash in swings the market that takes longer than a few hours. In fact, some shifts in the market may take longer than two or three days. This is why you need to set up your position ahead of time. This is what we mean by being proactive.

As for position trading, this is a long-term approach. Now, in the world of investing, "long-term" is a rather broad term. In some cases, there are investors who choose to hold on to positions for years. They are keen on holding on to the stock of prime companies as a means of preserving their wealth. Additionally, holding on to stocks for extended time periods enables investors to collect dividends from profits. For the purpose of this book, we are going to be looking at position investing as a long-term approach that spans any period greater than a week. Typically, most position investors hold open positions for periods ranging from a week to roughly 200 days. Later on, we'll discuss the fundamentals of this timeframe in great detail.

Benefits of Day Trading

Day trading can be an excellent way of supplementing your income. At first, you shouldn't expect it to replace your primary source(s) of income. Nevertheless, day trading can provide you with the extra income you need to pay down debt, save up for important purchases, or eventually make a career switch. Beyond this, there are clear benefits to day trading.

Consider these:

- Day trading is flexible. This means that you can trade anytime, anywhere.
- There is no limit to your potential income. When you master the fundamentals, you will find there is no market cap. You can make as much as you possibly can.
- There is no need for large investment capital. You don't need to invest thousands, or even millions, to get started. Just a few hundred dollars is enough to get started.
- It's fully automated. The trading platforms that you will be using are fully automated. This means that everything you need to do is there on your computer.

- You have access to a wide range of stocks and other financial products. You are only limited by your understanding of the products you are looking to trade.
- You don't pay commissions on each trade. There are costs per trade and maintenance fees. However, you cut out the middleman as there is no need to pay stockbrokers.

On the surface, day trading has a number of advantages. By taking full advantage of them, you can watch your capital grow quickly and easily. Best of all, you don't need to make any sacrifices to get started.

Drawbacks of Day Trading

As with anything, there are also drawbacks. This means that there are things you need to look out for. Nevertheless, day trading can be a great way for you to make money if you are wary of the following drawbacks.

- There are fees to be paid. These pertain to maintenance fees for the trading platform you are using in addition to the fees per trade that you need to pay. If you take advantage of bundles and other special offers, you can reduce the costs associated with trading.
- You have to pay taxes. Yes, there are taxes that need to be paid on the profits you make. So, it's best to take a look at what taxes you

may be liable for in your state. Generally speaking, you'll be on the hook for capital gains tax. So, do keep an eye out for this.

- Time and study are needed to master the craft. Yes, you will have to invest time and effort in learning the ropes of day trading. Still, it's time well spent. If you have a busy lifestyle, then it's important to take this into account before signing up.

- There is always risk involved in trading. When you engage in day trading or any type of investing, there is always risk involved. This is why studying trading is important as it will help you to manage the potential risk that may come from investing.

Through careful study and attention, you can compensate for these drawbacks. In fact, you can transform them into new opportunities. So, do take the time to evaluate these drawbacks, so you are not caught off-base.

Day Trading Equities

The term "equities" refers to stocks. As such, when you day trade equities, you are focusing specifically on stocks. While this means that you can branch out to other types of financial assets, the main focus of your investment endeavors is stocks. Of course, the world of stocks is quite large. There is any number of companies and industries you can focus on. That why it's important to narrow your focus on a group of stocks or a sector that you feel comfortable dealing with.

In this regard, many day traders narrow their focus on a single industry when first starting out. Since there is a considerable number of companies in the market, trying to capture them all can be quite difficult. So, some investors like to focus on tech companies. Others like to focus on manufacturing, retail, or even gas and oil. When you narrow your focus to a single industry or group of stocks, you facilitate your understanding of the dynamics in that particular sector. This makes it easier for you to gain specific insight into the movements in prices for these specific companies.

Other investors choose to focus on specific stock indices. A stock index is a grouping of stocks by industry, size, or turn of business. The largest stock index in the United States is the Dow Jones Industrial Average. The Dow Jones is a collection of the 30 largest publicly-traded companies in America. Its purpose is to track the performance of these companies and translate their performance into a round number that investors can visualize. This is the number that you see on the nightly news. For example, the Dow reached a high of over 29,000 points in February of 2020. This marked a new record for the Dow.

Other major stock indices include the NASDAQ. This index groups the major tech companies in the United States. Also, the S&P 500 is a collection of the 500 biggest companies traded in America. There are several other indices that you can use as a reference. However, the three mentioned in this chapter are the industry standard and serve a yardstick for investors. If you are keen on tracking one of these indices, you can do so as a means of giving you a specific target to shoot for. Otherwise, you may find yourself trying to cast a wide net. In the world of investing, that's not necessarily a good thing.

Day Trading Options

Options are both a tool and an instrument. The term "options" refers to a very specific type of contract in which investors set a number of parameters that guide a transaction. For instance, a common parameter is time. This means that investors set a specific time limit for a transaction to happen. A common timeframe is 30 days. This means that the transaction, be it buy or sell, will be activated at the 30-day mark.

The purpose of an option is to agree on price and/or quantity in advance of a deal taking place. This allows investors to lock in a certain price or amount, thereby giving them the assurance that they have the assets they need at the specified time or price. It's also important to note that a common parameter for options is price. Thus, a transaction may be triggered by a certain price point. This implies that if a stock hits a certain price, a buy or sell order is automatically enacted.

As a day trader, you can buy and sell these contracts for a price. Likewise, you can take out one of these contracts in order to hedge your position, particularly in uncertain times. The great thing about an options contract is that you don't actually have to go through with it. This is why it's called an "option." If you should choose not to go through with the deal, even when the specific parameters have been reached, all you would lose is the cost for underwriting the contract.

Day Trading FOREX

FOREX is the largest and most liquid market in the world. In this market, you are literally buying and selling currencies. The dynamic in this market is rather different from that of the stock market as you are dealing with the currency of sovereign nations. This means that there are socioeconomic factors that influence the valuation of currency in addition to the fundamental market forces. Still, FOREX is an exciting market that offers investors very short-term gains. Often, FOREX traders open and sell positions within a matter of minutes. However, in those few minutes, they can make a substantial gain.

It should be noted that "volume" is the name of the game in FOREX. The reason for this is due to the fact that you may only make pennies on each trade. But the size of your position is what amplifies the gains. Moreover, if you engage in high-frequency trading, that is, make a large number of transactions in a short timeframe, you can rack up small gains to the point where they are considerably large.

Also, FOREX is a 24-hour market. This means that it never closes. This is why many day traders also choose to engage in FOREX; it gives them the opportunity to continue trading even after the stock exchanges have closed. For those who have full-time jobs or busy schedules, FOREX offers an opportunity to trade at any time they choose. This is why FOREX is truly the weapon of choice for busy investors.

Chapter 2: Essentials of Day Trading

Once you have made up your mind to begin day trading, the next step is to begin doing research on how you can get started. Getting started is relatively easy. Gaining access to the market doesn't require a great deal of work. In fact, it's a rather easy process. The hard part is learning the ropes of the trading system that you will be using.

In this chapter, we are going to be focusing on the essentials of day trading. This means that we are going to be discussing what you need to do to get ready for your very first trade. Please bear in mind that day trading requires some careful study and learning early on. But once you get the hand of the trading system, it will be rather easy for you to navigate the waters of the trading world.

The hardest part of day trading is the research that does into determining the right stocks to pick and which are the best options for you to make money. This is important to note as not all stocks are created equal. The so-called "blue chip" stocks belong to companies that have a great track record. These are companies that have a long-lasting reputation and proven performance. As such, they are expensive and highly sought-after. Consequently, it's important for you to be careful with penny stocks. These are companies whose share price is less than five dollars. These stocks generally belong to companies that have serious financial or administrative issues but are yet to be liquidated. In essence, they are hanging on for dear life.

When you commit to regular research and study surrounding stocks, you will find that it's quite straightforward to pick winners from losers. The challenge then becomes entering and exiting trades at the right time. Learning to time your movements within trades is usually a matter of practice and experience. As you become familiar with the technical analysis tools that you can use to interpret price action, you'll be able to ascertain when to entre and when to leave. As a result, you can quickly "time" your moves so that you can make money every time.

To get started as a day trader, you need to open a brokerage account. This account will enable you to enter the trading floor (albeit virtually) so that you can begin buying and selling stocks.

Opening a New Brokerage Account

It's important to note that you need to open a brokerage account to trade stocks. This is an essential requirement as an average individual is not licensed to trade stocks. That's what stockbrokers are licensed to do. In addition, you can't simply turn on your computer to buy and sell stocks. To do this, you need to comply with government regulations. These regulations state that only duly licensed financial institutions can actively engage in trading stocks. Therefore, you need to trade through one of these institutions. Otherwise, you won't be able to gain access.

When you open a new account, what you are getting is access to the trading platform. This is the digital space in which traders can interact with one another. This is where all of the action takes place. As a result, you are granted access to this digital space by the financial institution that's running the trading platform.

There are no formal requirements for you to gain access to a day trading platform. The fact is that all you need is to meet the technical requirements of the trading platform and, most importantly, meet the financial requirements of the account you wish to open. Generally speaking, trading accounts can range from as little as $500 to several thousand depending on the level you wish to trade. As a novice investor, it's best to stay away from an account, requiring a large investment capital upon startup. It's better to open up an account that has a low investment capital requirement. The reason for this is simple. When you sink too much money into day trading when you are inexperienced, you may either be too cautious or too brazen. So, it's best to start off small and work your way up. If you are already experienced and have a larger sum on money, you can definitely try your hand at a larger investment capital position early on.

When you go about picking the institution you are going to do business with. Please keep in mind that you'll find one of two types of institutions. First, you have a full-service financial broker and second, a discount broker. The difference between them can be quite significant.

A full-service broker provides users with a full range of services. These services include the use of the trading platform in addition to a host of services such as real-time data, analytics, and other expert advice. In some cases, free training sessions are offered as part of the package. But the most important thing you should look for is the free demo account. When you sign up for a full account, you generally get a free trial account in which you can have access to the entire platform without using your capital. This means that you can trade with monopoly money for a few days.

This is something you need to take advantage of. By using the demo account, you'll be able to make mistakes without being concerned about blowing your investment capital. It's a great way to learn the ropes and be ready for the real thing.

As far as costs are concerned, full-service accounts generally come with an annual membership fee. While this fee may be waived when you sign up, you'll eventually have to pay some kind of maintenance fee. That's what keeps the lights on for these platforms. Additionally, you'll have to pay a fee per trade. When you deal with these types of brokers, the fees per trade are usually low. They will range anywhere from a few cents per trade to about a couple of dollars. It's important for you to be aware of how much you would be paying per trade. That way, you can manage your costs and calculate your real profits.

Then there are discount brokers. Discount brokers sell you access to the bare-bones platform. So, you can use the fully functional platform but without the bells and whistles. This usually means no access to analytics or real-time data. You'll have access to charts and graphs, but they are generally on a delay. So, you'll have to find another information service that can give you access to real-time data. It should also be noted that discount brokers have very low membership fees (in some cases they don't), but you'll need to keep a certain minimum balance in your account (which can be a bit high at times) while also a higher fee per trade. Be on the lookout for these fees per trade as they can be quite high at times. However, most discount brokers sell trade bundles. For instance, you'll get 10 trade for $2.99. Take advantage of these bundles as they'll help you keep your costs in check.

Another important thing about discount brokers is that they don't always allow you to have the demo account. So, if you are keen on starting out with a discount broker, please note that you will go live right from the start. As such, you need to be ready to trade for real.

Placing Your First Trades

Once you have gone about choosing your broker and trading system platform, you are ready to make your first trades. Making trades is a pretty straightforward process. You buy low and sell high. That's the logic behind it. However, the process itself can be a bit tricky. So, it's important to learn the basics of placing your first trades

In this section, we are going to look at how you can make your first trades happen. Please bear in mind that doing the tutorial until you are completely familiar with the dynamics of the trading system platform is essential. Otherwise, you won't be able to get the most out of the tools available to you.

Bid price

The first thing to note when placing a trade is the price action that occurs among investors and traders. Everyone has their own agenda, so to speak. What this means is that buyers want to get the lowest price will sellers want to get the highest price they can. Eventually, both parties meet somewhere in the middle. When this occurs, a transaction happens. And yes, there are times when they can't meet in the middle. In those cases, transactions stall until someone budges or orders are withdrawn.

With that in mind, the bid price is the price that buyers put up for a specific stock they want to purchase. The term "bid" is used as this is not the final price they are willing to pay. This is merely an offer that buyers make. In a manner of speaking, it's like an auction. If the seller is willing to take that price, then a match is made.

Most buyers are comfortable with the idea of going a bit higher if they believe they will find value at a higher price point. Then again, there are instances in which buyers panic and are willing to pay anything for an asset. If you are the holder in this situation, you can set your price and get paid accordingly. Also, bid prices are a reflection of what investors believe an asset is worth. So, don't be surprised if you see buyers paying far lower amounts than you might expect based on market averages.

Ask price

As for ask prices, well, the term speaks for itself; it's an asking price. In the ask price, sellers establish a price they would like to get for the stock they hold. If there is a match, then the sale occurs. If the price is not matched by any other investors, then the order goes unfulfilled. Therefore, the ask price is a parameter just like the bid price is. In the end, the convergence of both prices is what makes the market function.

It should be noted that in a healthy market, there is very little divergence among prices. This means that the price action is relatively stable. Naturally, there are fluctuations in the market. But on the whole, there is very little change. So, investors have a predictable range in which prices move. This is called a "range." As such, trading within a range can offer you the opportunity to make predictable gains. All you have to do is recognize the signals.

Best Time to Trade

In the world of day trading, the bulk of the action is generally clumped into two separate moments. These are the moments in which trading volume picks up. By "trading volume," we are referring to the number of transactions that take place during a specific timeframe. As such, there are specific times of day in which trading volume increases while there are other times when the action settles down. When you recognize these times, you can make a certain profit from them.

The best times to trade are right at the opening and closing of the trading. The reason for this is the increased trading volume. Think about it this way: if you go fishing, your chance of catching fish would be when the stream is busiest and not when it's quietest. This is the same logic that applies here.

Before the start of the trading day, most investors set up their positions so that they are quickly carried out when trading officially opens. This is where the flood of orders comes in. The flood of orders is based on the previous day's close. For instance, is the stock of company ASD closed lower than usual, there might be a flood of purchase orders at the beginning of the next trading day. This is a point where you could get in on the action. By the same token, if the price of ASD closed higher than normal, there might be a flurry of sell order at the outset of the day. As such, it would be a bad time to get in. Rather, it would be best to get in after the action has died down.

At the end of the trading day, most investors look to liquidate their positions. So, it's a perfect time to sell. If you are holding any open positions, you can set up your trades so that they go through during the final hour or so, leading up to the close of the markets. That way, you can make some profits at the tail end of the day while ensuring that you close all positions before wrapping up for the day.

This is the dynamic of day trading in a nutshell. Throughout the day, you can open positions if the price is right while also enabling you to make profits should conditions be favorable. A good rule of thumb to keep in mind is that there is no reason why you should enter a trade unless you are sure about what you are doing. If you are unsure about anything, it's always best to stay away. You would be better off sitting out a trade rather than taking a plunge and getting hammered.

Risk Management

Risk is an inherent part of trading. There is no question that any type of investing comes with its dose of risk. This implies that you need to be mindful of the role risk plays in your investment activity. On the whole, risk is about understanding what could go wrong and what you can do to remedy it. Therefore, your understanding of these conditions will help you to avoid catastrophic mistakes.

So, let's take a look at five helpful rules when considering risk in your day trading endeavors:

1. **Don't put all your eggs in one basket**. When you put too many of your resources into a single trade, you are opening up the door to trouble. So, it's best to limit your exposure to risk by setting a maximum amount of funds invested in a single trade.

2. **Invest in companies you are familiar with**. If you plan on investing in a company you have never heard of, you might be asking for trouble. So, always make sure that you do a cursory check on any company you're thinking about trading.

3. **Avoid following the herd**. When you hear folks talking about the hottest stock at the moment, you're already too late. The best time to trade stocks is when no one is talking about them. You can figure out what these stocks are by doing your research.

4. **Be careful with the "fear of missing out**. Often, you hear investors talking about the next big thing. So, it's natural to assume that if you don't get in, you're going to miss out on a great

opportunity. However, there comes a time when you get into an asset just because you're afraid if you don't, others will think you're crazy. This is why you need to make your own decisions, even if that means going against the herd.

5. **Make sure you check out the broker you are doing business with**. Always ensure that when you sign up for a new investment account, you double-check on the broker you have chosen. If you find that there's something shady or not quite right about them, don't sign up. It's better to be skeptical rather than getting burned.

Golden Rules of Money Management

In order to hedge risk, you need to follow the golden rules of money management. So, here are three rules which have proven to stand the test of time. By following them, you can ensure that your portfolio will be safe and sound.

1. **Limit your positions to 1% or 2% of your total investment capital**. This rule calls for moderation. So, never place more than 2% of your total portfolio on a single trade. While you can invest the entire sum of your capital, make sure it stays under the 2% threshold on individual trades.

2. **Cut your losses**. When a deal goes south, always make sure to exit before you dig yourself deeper into the hole. Whenever you try to hold on just a little bit longer in hopes of having the price bounce back, you may end up losing more money in the process. So, as

soon as you see prices heading south, cut your losses. You'll be able to make up those losses later on.

3. **Keep cool**. It's very easy to let your emotions get the best of you. For instance, you might find that you are quick to anger when you lose money on a deal. By the same token, you might think you are invincible when you go on a hot streak. By keeping a level head, you'll be able to make objective decisions every time you enter a deal.

With these golden rules, you'll never go wrong. So, do your best to keep a level head. You'll find that it's easier to manage situations every time the action gets hot and heavy.

Basic Technical Analysis Tools for Day Traders

Technical analysis is the study of the behavior of stocks through the use of quantitative analysis tools. These tools allow you to obtain objective information that you can use to make sound investment decisions. Without them, you would be basing your decisions on nothing more than hunches. So, it's best to do your best to utilize these tools. Here are three of the most important tools you will use to help you make sound decisions.

1. **Moving average**. The moving average is the average price of a stock over a given period of time. Most charts present the moving

average on a daily basis. This means that the price listed reflects the average price of the course of a trading day. The most common measures are the 20, 50, and 200-day moving average. By studying these measures, you'll be able to analyze the overall behavior of the stock's prices.

2. **Trend**. The trend is the direction in which price is heading. Trend can be bullish (increasing) or bearing (falling). When you are able to identify trends, you'll be able to see where the price of the stock is heading. This can be an indication that it's time to buy or it's time to sell. Charting software will calculate this automatically for you. So, make sure you see this line whenever you look at charts.

3. **Significant levels**. These levels refer to the "ceiling" and the "floor" of a stock's price. The ceiling, or resistance level, is a psychological barrier that is reflected in the maximum price that investors are willing to pay. When you look at a chart, you'll notice a resistance level when the price of the stock seems to reach a certain mark and then fall back down. By the same token, a floor, or support level, the lowest level a stock's price will fall. This means that investors feel that this is the lowest price for that stock. Therefore, they buy when the price reaches this point. In other words, this is the lowest point a stock's price will reach during the timeframe you are analyzing.

These three tools are essential in evaluating a stock you are looking to buy. The moving average will help you determine both trend and significant levels. With this, you will be able to determine the entry and exit points of your trades. At the end of the day, you'll be able to make informed decisions regarding the deals you plan to make.

Using the moving average to enter and exit a trade

A simple way in which you could use the moving average to enter and exit a trade is called the "crossover" strategy. In this strategy, you need to pay attention to the price of the stock itself and the moving average. When the actual price of the stock crosses over the moving average, you have a signal of a potential trend reversal. Depending on the nature of the reversal, it would either be time to get in out get out.

- In a bearish trend, if the price becomes higher than the moving average, then you have signal in which the bearish trend may suddenly turn into a bullish one. This would be the time to buy. That way, you can capitalize on the gains that rising, bullish trend would make. The ideal time to buy would be right at the point of crossover. To do this, you need to track the moving average and the current price of the stock. When this cross over occurs, you can place your trade and catch the upswing.
- In a bullish trend, if the price dips below the moving average, then you have a signal of a potential downturn. In this case, you need to pay close attention to the actual point in which the price falls under the moving average. When this occurs, you are at the right time to sell. This is the highest point in the trend. Therefore, if you wait any longer, you will miss out on potential gains.

It should be noted that the most common measure taken here is the 20-day moving average. However, you could compare the 10-day, 20-day and 50-day moving averages to get confirmation of trend reversal.

Chapter 3: Choosing the Best Stocks for Your Portfolio

Knowing how to choose the right stocks is an art form. Many gurus have made their livelihood claiming they know the right stocks to purchase at any given time. In fact, they are keen on pointing out when you should buy and when you should sell. They don't all have perfect track records, but some get it right more often than not.

The issue with picking stocks is that you don't really know if these gurus have an agenda. After all, who knows if they are being paid to promote their own stocks? This is true quite often. You find these gurus promoting companies that they have some kind of stake in. So, you should always take stock advice with a grain of salt.

In this chapter, we are going to focus on the tools you can use to make your own stock picks. Best of all, you don't need to depend on so-called "expert" advice. In fact, all you need is reliable data. Then, with the right analytical tools, you can go ahead and make fairly accurate assumptions based on the information you see. That makes stock picking a fairly straightforward process.

Company Financials

All good investors need to have a solid understanding of company financials. Now, it helps if you have an accounting degree. But you don't need one in order to understand the major points of a company's financials. On the whole, there are two financial statements you need to become familiar with: a balance sheet and a profit and loss statement. Other financial statements are important, but they aren't nearly as important as these two.

The reason why the balance sheet is so important is that it provides a general overview of a company's financial situation. In that statement, you can find the overall health and growth potential. Any possible issues will be reflected in this statement, for instance, high levels of debt. As for the profit and loss (P&L) statement, you will find that it shows how much money the company is making and how much it's actually profiting. This is important to note as there are companies with enormous revenues but very poor profits.

From these two statements, you can use the following financial indicators to determine the health and growth potential of a company. If you are keen on doing your research, you may find some hidden gems that might have been overlooked by other investors.

Company revenue

This indicator is quite useful in determining a company's health. However, it's not an exact measure as not all companies have similar earnings. Naturally, some companies earn a lot more than others. In this regard, a good comparison would be within the industry that the company operates in. For instance, you are evaluating a mining stock. So, it's important to compare the company you are studying with others in the same sector.

Additionally, revenue needs to grow in order for a company to show potential. If you find that revenue is stagnant, then there has to be a reason for this. If you cannot find a logical reason for it, then chances are the company is being mismanaged. In this case, it's best to stay away. A good, healthy growth rate is anything above 10% annually. Although, be careful if a company shows astronomical growth rates. Yes, they look great in the short run but are most likely unsustainable in the long term. This is why looking at companies with a solid track record always makes the most sense. If you are looking at a relatively new company, then be wary.

Earnings Per Share

This indicator provides a much clearer picture of where a company is headed. Simply put, earnings per share refers to the profit divided by the number of shares outstanding. Now, this indicator is not the same as dividends. Dividends are a percentage of after-tax profits that are distributed to shareholders. Earnings per share are just a gross measure of the profits divided by the number of shares. This helps provide a better indication of what shareholders can expect in terms of the company's performance.

When looking at this indicator, you can get a much more even comparison across all companies as profits are universal regardless of the cash amounts. So, if a company is making a 20% profit, this is a measure that can be compared with other companies across the board.

Return on Equity

"Equity" is the accounting term for capital; in other words, the number of resources a company has invested in its production processes. This indicator is simple yet effective in determining the overall performance of a company. All you need to do is that the after-tax profit and divide it by the company's equity. So, if the company profited $100 and has a total equity of $100, then the company is obtaining a return of $1 for every $1 of equity. This would be a phenomenal return. Generally speaking, the dollar amount for this indicator is pennies on the dollars' worth of equity. Nevertheless, it allows investors and analysts to judge the efficiency with which equity is being utilized in the company.

Analyst Recommendations

Analysts and financial experts are always weighing in on company performance. In particular, there is the "earnings season," in which companies published the audited financial statements. This season occurs several times a year. Each season coincides with the end of every quarter. For instance, Q4 earnings are reported in early February of the following year. Q1 earnings are reported in late April, while Q2 earnings are posted in July. Q3 is reported in October. During this time, analysts pour over the data for major companies looking for cracks. By the same token, analysts also look for positive signals. From here, recommendations are issued. You may find recommendations such as "buy," "sell," or "hold." However, always double-check on what you hear. Don't take experts at face value as you never know if they are off base in their assessments.

Positive earnings

Whenever companies post positive earnings, analysts tend to give them a favorable review. However, if the overall trend indicates that earnings are on the way down, then analysts may issue a warning. This often occurs with large corporations that are subject to changes in the market. As such, analysts may tell investors to proceed with caution.

In the event that a company posts negative earnings for a quarter, analysts may sound the alarm bells. After all, if there is no indication that the company may recover, analysts may recommend investors to abandon ship. So, always be on the lookout for reports during earnings seasons. You may end up running into some truly unexpected surprises.

Earnings forecast

This is a key element that influences the opinions of investors. Earnings forecasts can be issued in one of two ways. First, there is "forward guidance" that is issued by company directors. Forward guidance is what companies tell their investors to expect. In some cases, forward guidance may be bullish; that is, the company's directors expect positive results moving forward. In other cases, forward guidance may indicate caution as company directors may be expecting difficulties ahead.

The other source of forecasts comes from analysts who crunch the numbers. They may see things that the company itself may be unwilling to admit. As a result, analysts would go about issuing their own guidance for investors.

When investors compare both types of forecasts, they can make up their minds about the direction that a company is headed. Now, it should be noted that opinions do not generally diverge; that is, the company is bullish while analysts are bearish. Where opinions generally diverge is in the nature of the direction the company is headed. For example, is analysts believe a company is in trouble, they may be rather serious about it while the company may seem to downplay the situation.

Whenever you are researching a stock, always look for any forward guidance and analysts' forecasts. These elements can help you paint a picture of where that company may be headed in the long run. This could offer you enough forewarning.

Earnings growth

As mentioned earlier, earnings present the best indicator of where a company is headed. When evaluating the potential of a company, always look at the historical growth of a company, and then compare it to projected growth. This comparison should provide you with a clear indication of what to expect. For instance, if a company has demonstrated consistent growth at 5%, a sudden forecast of 20% wouldn't make sense unless there was a valid reason. If this reason is due to something like a new product launch, then you may buy into the hype. However, always be wary of any promises. Companies that have a proven track record of successful product launches can cash in on the expectation of a new product. But those that don't have a good track record may leave investors uncertain about its future earnings.

Other Financial Indicators

Here are other indicators that you can use to evaluate the potential for investing in a company. They will always come in handy, particularly when you are unfamiliar with the company itself. Please bear in mind that all of this information is usually available to the public. So, you won't have to crunch the numbers yourself.

1. **PEG Ratio.** The Price/Earnings to Growth Ratio is used to measure the trade-off that exists among the price, the earnings per share, and the expected growth of the company. In general, the PEG should be much higher than the company's actual growth. The rule of thumb here is that a PEG Ration over 1 indicates a company is overvalued while a PEG less than 1 indicates the company is undervalued. This is a good indication of the way investors feel about a particular stock as the price reflects this sentiment.

2. **Industry price earnings.** It is also important to take a look at the earnings across the industry. This is a fair comparison as you can use the industry leaders as a good yardstick for what you can expect from individual companies. If you find that companies are on par, then you have a balanced industry. If you find that a small group of companies dominate the market, then smaller players may not have a lot of room for growth unless they are disruptive, meaning that they can be game-changers.

3. **Dividend**. A dividend is what a company pays out to its shareholders at the end of a fiscal year. This is a percentage that is based on the total after-tax profit of the company. When a company is in trouble, it may choose to suspend its dividend payment either by withholding it, that is paying it out at a later date, or simply not paying it. While the latter is a rather unpopular decision, it can be done to help the company save money while it stabilizes. It should be noted that when a company files for bankruptcy protection, all dividends are suspended.

Please keep in mind that a company's financials are like a blood test for a sick patient. The bloodwork done a patient will reveal what problems the patient might be facing. As such, financial statements provide a similar measure for companies. If the company is in trouble, its financials will reveal this. Of course, there is always the possibility that companies may get creative with their accounting. This is why you need to do your homework on what companies are doing.

On the whole, you can save yourself a great deal of problems by double-checking the facts. It could be that you believed a company was healthy when, in reality, they had issues brewing beneath the surface. Please bear in mind that successful traders and investors are always on the lookout for any information that may tip them off as to what they can expect. So, it's always a good idea to keep your eyes and ears open.

Conclusion

Thank you very much for making it all the way through this book. We hope that you have gotten a clear picture of what it means to be an investor by this point. On the whole, being an investor is about building wealth and then taking the necessary steps to preserve it. After all, what good would it do to build your wealth only to lose it?

When you are new to investing, it can be quite tough to sort through the various kinds of information that are available to you. As a result, books such as this one will provide a beacon that you can follow on your road to becoming an investor and not just a consumer. At the end of the day, you will have everything you need to become highly successful. The only thing that you need is to make up your mind that you are committed to your new way of life.

We have outlined the steps that you need to take in order to get started. So, the time has come for you to get to work. If you are truly ready to get started in the world of investing, be it as a passive or active investor, make the commitment to devote your attention to building your wealth. With the tools in this book, you can get there.

So, what's the next step?

Please go over any of the sections in this book that you feel you need to further your knowledge. Then, set out to build your personal strategy. You will find that building this strategy will help guide you throughout your journey as an investor.

Thank you once again for reading this book. If you have found it to be useful, please tell your friends, family, and colleagues about it. They will surely find it useful, too!

www.ingramcontent.com/pod-product-compliance
Lightning Source LLC
LaVergne TN
LVHW010405070526
838199LV00065B/5897